# SPIDER-MAN™

Based on the screenplay by
David Koepp

Based on the Marvel Comic Book
by Stan Lee and Steve Ditko

LEVEL 1

SCHOLASTIC

**Adapted by:** Jane Rollason

**Commissioning Editor:** Helen Parker

**Editor:** Clare Gray

**Cover layout:** Emily Spencer

**Designer:** Victoria Wren

**Picture research:** Emma Bree

**Photo credits:**
Cover image and inside photos provided courtesy
Columbia Pictures Industries, Inc.
Page 32: C. Stone, S. Ditko/Marvel/Corbis.
Page 34: DigitalVision.
Page 35: eStockphoto, M. Del Grosso/Alamy.
Page 36: E. Thompson/Corbis; J. Levy/Getty Images.
Page 37: J. L. Gerome Ferris/Superstock.



Published by Scholastic Ltd 2007



Printed in Singapore

# CONTENTS

**Peter Parker** lives with Uncle Ben and Aunt May. When he was four, his mother and father died in a car crash. He loves Mary Jane (MJ), the girl next door. But can he ever tell her?

**Spider-Man** lives to help the people of New York. He moves like a spider. He can run up walls and 'fly' through the sky.

**Mary Jane Watson (MJ)** lives with her family in the house next to Peter's. She doesn't know Peter loves her. Or *maybe* she knows …

**The Green Goblin** is strong and clever, like Spider-Man. But he doesn't care about the people of New York.

# MAN™

**Norman Osborn** is a scientist and the head of OsCorp (the Osborn Corporation). He is very rich and lives for his work.

**Harry Osborn** lives with his father Norman Osborn in a big house. Peter is Harry's best friend. Peter helps Harry with his science work.

**Aunt May** and **Uncle Ben** are good and kind. When Peter's mother and father died, they gave Peter a home. Peter is like a son to them.

# PLACES

Spider-Man's story happens in **New York**.
**Manhattan Island** is the centre of New York. You can find the biggest and most important buildings here.
**Fifth Avenue** is a famous street in Manhattan.
**Times Square** is on 42nd Street. It is right at the centre of Manhattan.
**The Queensboro Bridge** goes between Manhattan and Queens.
Aunt May and Uncle Ben live outside Manhattan, in **Forest Hills**.

# Chapter 1
# The girl and the spider

Peter Parker lived next door to Mary Jane Watson (MJ). They went to the same school. Peter liked MJ a lot, but he never told her. She already had a boyfriend. His name was Flash. He was good-looking and he was the school's top football player.

One day their class went to the Columbia Genetic Research Institute*. Peter was late. He ran behind the bus, then at last it stopped. He was red and hot and everyone laughed at him. As Peter walked down the bus, Flash put his foot out. Peter crashed to the floor. Everyone laughed louder.

The bus arrived at the Institute. Harry Osborn wasn't on the bus. He arrived in a big car – a Rolls Royce – with his father and a driver.

Harry was new to the school and he wasn't good at science. Peter was fantastic at science and he often helped Harry. They were good friends.

'Peter, this is my father,' said Harry.

'Ah, the great scientist!' said Norman Osborn. 'I'm a scientist too. Your mother and father must be happy!' said Mr Osborn.

'I live with Uncle Ben and Aunt May,' said Peter. 'Yes, they are happy.'

'Hey, you two!' called the teacher, 'Let's go!'

A woman took the class to see some spiders.

* *A science school – part of Columbia University*

'There are 32,000 different spiders in the world,' she said, '… and these. These fifteen spiders are special. We took the best bits from three different spiders and put them together.'

'There are only fourteen,' said MJ.

'Oh,' said the woman. 'Maybe someone is doing some work on Number 15.'

Peter took some photos of MJ with the spiders for the school newspaper.

'Ow! What was that?' he thought. The back of his hand was red. And there on the floor was … a spider. *The* spider! Spider Number 15.

'Parker, let's go!' said the teacher.

## Chapter 2
## The special gas

Norman Osborn arrived at OsCorp*. Important buyers were there that day. First they looked at Osborn's new glider. The glider worked beautifully. But the buyers

* *Mr Osborn's big scientific workplace*

didn't want the glider. They asked questions about OsCorp's special gas.

'It makes you very, very strong,' said Dr Stromm, Osborn's top scientist. 'But it can also make you very angry and crazy,' he said. 'We need more tests.'

'The gas must be ready in two weeks,' said the buyers. 'We need it then.'

Norman Osborn and Dr Stromm were at OsCorp late that evening.

'I'm going to test the gas. It must work.'

'No, Mr Osborn,' said Stromm. 'The gas isn't ready yet. Give me two more weeks.'

'Two weeks is too late,' said Osborn. 'Just start it when I'm ready.'

Osborn went into a special room. Stromm closed the doors after him and started the gas.

Soon there was green gas everywhere in the room. Osborn tried to shout. Stromm stopped the gas. But it was too late – Osborn was dead!

Stromm ran into the room. Suddenly Osborn's eyes opened. He was a different man now. His body was very strong. And he was very angry. He took Stromm in his hands. In seconds, Stromm was dead.

Peter had a terrible night. When he woke up, he thought, 'Am I dead?' Slowly he started to move.

'No!' he said, 'I feel fantastic!' His body was beautiful and very strong. He looked across the room. 'I can see much better, too.' This was a new Peter Parker.

Later that day Peter was in the lunch-room at school. MJ sat with Flash a few tables behind Peter.

'My hands feel different,' Peter thought. He looked closer at his right hand. Suddenly, a line of spider-webbing shot from his hand across the room. It shot onto some food on the next table. Peter watched the food fly across the room. It hit Flash! He turned and saw Peter. 'Parker!'

Peter ran out of the lunch-room but Flash followed him. Peter turned. Flash tried to hit him, but Peter moved too quickly. Flash tried again and again to hit Peter. Then Peter hit Flash. And he hit him right across the room!

Peter ran out of the school. He went down a street between two tall buildings. He wanted to test his new body. He went up a wall. He went higher and higher. At the top he looked down at the road with its little cars. Then he ran and jumped from building to building.

'Whoohoo!' he shouted.

He stopped on one building.

'Now,' he thought, 'I'm going to try this spider-webbing.'

He put his hands in front of him and looked at the building opposite. At first nothing happened. Then long lines of strong webbing shot from his hands.

He took a line of the webbing and jumped. 'Woohoo! Now I can fly!'

Peter came home late that night. He heard shouts from MJ's house. He went into the garden. MJ's back door opened. MJ walked into her garden and saw Peter.

'Did you hear that?' she asked.

'No ... er ... well, I heard something.'

'You can always hear us, right?' Then she smiled. 'So, school finishes soon. What's next for you?'

'I want to live in Manhattan. I want to be a photographer. What about you?'

'Yeah, I'm going to live in the city, too. I want a job on Broadway*.'

* *A famous street in New York. You can see lots of plays and music shows here.*

'You were great in all those school plays. I cried when you were Cinderella,' he said.

'Peter! We were six then!'

A car stopped in front of MJ's house. It was new and cool and it was Flash's car. MJ put on her party girl face and ran to the car.

## Chapter 3
## The worst day

Peter thought a lot about MJ and about Flash's car. He wanted a cool car, too. The next evening, Peter ran to the front door. He had some things in a bag.

'I'm going into town. I want to finish some schoolwork,' he called.

'Wait!' said Uncle Ben. 'Let's go in the car.'

Uncle Ben stopped the car.

'Thanks for the ride,' smiled Peter.

'Let's talk,' said Uncle Ben.

'I haven't got time right now.'

'That fight you had at school – with Flash.'

'I didn't start the fight,' said Peter.

'I know,' said Uncle Ben. 'But this is an important time. You're changing into a man. Be careful, Peter! *With great power comes great responsibility*.*'

Peter was angry. He opened the car door.

'I know I'm not your father …' said Uncle Ben.

'No. You're not!' shouted Peter.

Uncle Ben went quiet.

'See you here at ten o'clock,' he said.

* *Peter must think carefully before he does something. And he must always do the right thing.*

Sadly, Peter watched Uncle Ben's car drive away.

Peter walked across the street to an old building. He went in and walked into a big room. There were many people there. They watched a fight with two men. One of the men was very big and ugly. His name was Bone Saw McGraw. He jumped on top of the other man and the fight was over.

A few crazy people wanted to fight Bone Saw for money. Peter wanted to fight him, too. He needed the money. He took a costume and mask out of his bag.

'$3000 for three minutes with Bone Saw,' a man shouted. 'Let's hear a big shout for our next fighter ...' The man looked at Peter's costume – red and blue with spider-webs. ' ... for SPIDER-MAN!'

Everyone looked at Peter and laughed. Bone Saw had crazy eyes and a terrible smile. He was big and very strong.

The fight started. When Bone Saw tried to hit Peter, Peter jumped right over him. Then Bone Saw hit Peter with a chair and Peter hit the floor. Then Peter jumped up and hit Bone Saw. He knocked him out! Everybody shouted and laughed. They loved it!

After the fight, Peter went for his money. The man gave him $100.

'$100?' said Peter. 'It's $3000! Not $100!'

'It's $3000 for three minutes. Your fight was only two minutes.'

'I need that money,' said Peter.

'Not my problem,' said the man.

Peter walked away angrily. Then there was a shout behind him.

'Hey! Stop that man! He's got my money.'

A man with white hair ran to a door and out of the building.

'Why didn't you stop him?' the man asked Peter.

'Not my problem,' said Peter.

A few minutes later Peter was in the street. Some people were around the body of a man. Peter walked through the people. He saw Uncle Ben on the road.

'What happened?' asked Peter. 'It's my Uncle Ben.'

'Someone shot this old man and took his car,' said a woman.

Peter looked at the body. 'Uncle Ben!' he cried. 'Uncle Ben!'

Uncle Ben opened his eyes. Very quietly, he said, 'Peter.' And then he died.

'We can see the car. It's on Fifth Avenue,' said the police radio.

Peter ran between two buildings. He put on his costume. He went up one of the buildings. He used his webbing and jumped from building to building. Very soon he was on Fifth Avenue.

Then he saw Uncle Ben's car. He jumped on top of it. SMASH! He put his hand through the front window.

'Aaagh!' cried the driver and crashed the car. Peter followed the driver into a dark old building. Peter had the man in his hands. The man turned to the light and Peter saw his face. It was the man from the Bone Saw fight, the man with white hair. It was the worst day of Peter's life.

# Chapter 4
# An old life ends

Life was quiet after Uncle Ben died. Peter and Harry worked hard at school and soon their last year was over. Everyone's family came to school on the last day.

'Good news, Peter,' Harry said. 'My dad bought a flat for me in Manhattan. And there's a room for you.'

'That's great!' said Peter.

Then Harry's father arrived.

'You did it,' Mr Osborn said to Harry. He was a little surprised but also very happy. 'Good work!'

Then he turned to Peter. 'And Peter – the best science student in the school! That's fantastic!'

Mr Osborn looked at Peter. 'Life isn't easy for you

right now,' he said. 'Try to enjoy the day. It's the start of something new.' Then he smiled. 'You're almost a brother to Harry. That makes you family.'

Peter smiled back. But he was frightened. His 'spider sense' saw something terrible in Mr Osborn's eyes.

Harry saw MJ and Flash. MJ didn't look happy. Flash looked very angry. Then Flash walked away.

'It's over for MJ and Flash,' thought Harry. 'Good!'

Later that day, Peter sat quietly at home. He thought about Uncle Ben and he started to cry. Then he remembered Uncle Ben's words. '*With great power comes great responsibility*.' Something in Peter woke up.

'I'm strong,' he thought. 'And I'm a good person. I *must* help other people. Uncle Ben was right!'

## Chapter 5
## A new life starts

Spider-Man worked very hard. Every day terrible things happened in New York. Every day Spider-Man helped people. Soon, Spider-Man was big news in New York. All the newspapers had stories about him. But who was he? No one knew!

A few weeks later, Peter walked alone through the streets of Manhattan. Suddenly, he saw MJ come out of a restaurant.

'Hi, MJ!' he called.

'Hi!' she smiled. 'What are you doing around here?'
'I'm looking for a job,' he answered. 'What about you?'
'I'm ... I'm working on Broadway now,' she said.
'Hey, that's great, MJ. You're living your dream.'
But then a man came out of the restaurant. The man was angry with MJ. The day's money wasn't right – $6 wasn't there.
MJ shouted back at the man, then she turned to Peter.
'Some dream!' she said. 'I work here ...'
'There are worse jobs.'
'Don't tell Harry,' she said.
'Harry?'
'We're going out,' she said. 'Didn't he tell you?'
'Oh, yeah. Right!' he said.
MJ turned to go. 'Let's get together again sometime,' she smiled. And then she left.

Back at the flat, Peter was very sad. He didn't have a job and MJ was Harry's girlfriend now.
Then he saw the front of the *Daily Bugle* newspaper: '*$$$ FOR PHOTOS OF SPIDER-MAN!*'
Peter smiled. 'I know just the right man for the job!' he thought.

## Chapter 6
## The photographer

The next morning Peter went out with his Spider-Man costume and his camera. When bad things happened on the streets of New York, he put his camera up high. Then Spider-Man did his good work and the camera took the pictures.

Mr Jameson looked quickly at Peter's photos. He was the top man at the *Daily Bugle* newspaper. He *loved* the pictures, but he didn't say it.

'You can have $200,' he said.

'That's not much,' Peter answered.

'OK, $300,' said Mr Jameson. 'And bring me more!'

Peter left the newspaper building with $300. And the next day his photo of Spider-Man was on the front of the paper. Not bad for a morning's work!

All the important people at OsCorp sat around a table. Norman Osborn talked about OsCorp's good work.

'Quest Aerospace* is big, but we are bigger!' he said.

'That's great news, Norman,' said one of the men. 'Because of this, we are selling OsCorp.'

'What?' said Osborn.

* *Another big scientific corporation, like OsCorp.*

'Quest Aerospace is giving us a lot of money.'

'Why didn't you tell me?'

'They didn't want a big fight, and they don't want you.'

'You can't do this to me,' said Osborn. 'I started OsCorp. I gave everything to OsCorp!'

'That's true,' said Fargas, Osborn's Number 2. 'But we all want this. We're selling after the OsCorp World Unity Festival*. I'm sorry, Norman.'

The OsCorp World Unity Festival was a street party in Times Square. Lots of families were there. Peter was there for the *Daily Bugle* newspaper.

Fargas and the other OsCorp people watched from the first floor of a beautiful old building. Peter saw Harry and MJ there, too, but not Norman Osborn.

Suddenly Peter's spider sense screamed. He heard something in the sky. Everybody looked up. It was a green goblin on a glider – OsCorp's glider! The people stopped and watched the glider. It was fantastic!

The glider moved very fast through Times Square. The green rider laughed crazily. He moved close to Fargas and suddenly the wall of the building exploded. Everyone screamed. Fargas and the other OsCorp people were dead!

Peter looked for MJ. She wasn't dead. 'But she's going

* *OsCorp's street party for the people of New York.*

to fall!' thought Peter.

The Green Goblin came up close to MJ and laughed crazily. He had terrible yellow eyes and teeth. But then someone in red and blue crashed into the Green Goblin with his feet. It was Spider-Man!

Spider-Man went after the Green Goblin. Then Spider-Man and the Green Goblin started to fight. And the Goblin hit Spider-Man right across the street!

MJ screamed, 'Help! Help!'

Spider-Man heard her and jumped up. But the Green Goblin crashed into him – and they both crashed into a window. The Green Goblin hit Spider-Man. Then Spider-Man jumped down near to MJ. He shot webbing at the Goblin's face. Then he pulled some parts out of the glider. Part of the glider exploded. The Green Goblin took his glider up into the sky.

Suddenly MJ screamed again. Spider-Man jumped down to her. He shot webbing onto a building and pulled her into his arms. He was just in time!

He shot more webbing and moved from building

to building with MJ in his arms. MJ wasn't frightened – it was so exciting! He left her in a garden on top of a building.

'Wait!' she called. 'Who are you?'

'You know me. I'm Spider-Man!'

And then he wasn't there.

## Chapter 7
## 'We can work together'

That night, Norman Osborn was alone at home. He read the evening newspaper. There was a story about the OsCorp people. They were all dead.

'Who did it?' he thought.

'We did it.'

'Who said that?'

'You know,' came the answer.

Osborn looked around the empty room. 'Where are you?' he cried.

'I'm right here.'

He started to understand. It was in his head … it was him.

'Ha, ha, ha!' laughed the Green Goblin. 'This is only the start! Only one person can stop us … Or maybe he can work with us?'

And now Osborn knew. He *was* the Green Goblin!

The Green Goblin crashed through the window of the *Daily Bugle*.

'Who takes Spider-Man's photos?' he shouted. His hands were around Mr Jameson. Suddenly, Spider-Man was at the window.

'Put him down,' he shouted. But the Green Goblin shot sleeping gas into Spider-Man's face. Then he put Spider-Man on his glider and left the building quickly.

A little later, Spider-Man opened his eyes. He was on top of a tall building.

'Wake up, Spider-Man,' the Green Goblin said quietly. 'You're not dead. But you can't move. You are very special,

Spider-Man. You and I are not so different,' he said. 'We can work together … '

He jumped onto his glider.

'Think about it,' he said.

A week later, Peter went to find MJ. She came out of a building on Broadway.

'Hey, MJ,' called Peter, 'It's me again!'

'Hi, Peter.'

'Did they give you the part?' asked Peter.

'They didn't like me,' said MJ sadly.

'Let's go for a burger. You can have anything … up to $7.84.'

MJ laughed. 'I'd like that,' she said. 'Oh, but I'm going out to dinner with Harry. Come with us.'

'No, thanks,' said Peter.

MJ turned and walked away. It started to rain. She knew

a quick way and walked down a dark street.

Suddenly, four men were around her. She hit one and then another.

And suddenly he was there! Spider-Man shot webbing at the four men. He pulled them back from MJ. The men hit him, but Spider-Man was stronger. The men ran away and Spider-Man jumped onto a wall.

He came down the wall head first.

'You saved me again!' said MJ. 'You are fantastic! I want to thank you this time.'

MJ moved close to Spider-Man and they kissed slowly. Suddenly, the world stopped – it was a fantastic kiss.

On Thanksgiving Day*, Peter was on Sixth Avenue. A tall building was on fire.

'My little boy's in there!' a woman screamed. Spider-Man jumped up into the building. He saved the boy and gave him to his mother.

** An important holiday in America. People eat special food with their family and friends.*

Then they heard another scream.

'There's someone still up there,' a woman shouted.

Spider-Man jumped back into the building.

'Where are you?' he called.

Then he saw an old woman. The woman turned around. It was the Green Goblin!

'You!' said Peter.

'So, Spider-Man,' he said. 'Are we a team or not?'

'Not,' said Peter.

'No one says no to me!' shouted the Green Goblin. He hit Spider-Man hard. But Spider-Man jumped and hit him back. Then, there was an explosion. Spider-Man jumped out of a window and back into the street.

MJ, Aunt May and Norman Osborn were with Harry at his flat. It was time for Thanksgiving lunch. Peter walked in the door.

'Sorry I'm late,' he said.

Everyone sat down at the table. Mr Osborn looked very closely at Peter. Their eyes met for a few seconds. Then Mr Osborn jumped up from his chair.

'I must go,' he said quickly. 'I'm sorry, everyone.'

Harry followed his father out of the flat.

'What are you doing?' he asked angrily. 'What about MJ? She's important to me.'

'Harry, please. Look at her! Beautiful girls only like rich men for their money. Have fun with MJ and then forget her.'

The others heard everything.

Mr Osborn left and Harry came in.

'Well, Harry. You didn't say much for me, did you?' said MJ. 'Your father said some terrible things!'

'My father's a great man. You don't know anything about him.'

MJ walked to the door. 'I'm sorry, Aunt May,' she said. Then she walked out and closed the door behind her.

## Chapter 8
## The last fight

Late that night Aunt May was alone in her bedroom. She looked at a photo of Uncle Ben.

Suddenly, the bedroom wall exploded. The Green Goblin was there on his glider. He looked at her with his terrible yellow eyes and laughed crazily.

Peter ran to Aunt May's room at the hospital. She wasn't dead. Her face was white and she cried out, 'Those terrible yellow eyes!'

'What happened?' shouted Peter, but no one answered.

Peter stopped for a second. Then he understood.

'He knows!' he thought. 'The Green Goblin knows Aunt May. He knows Peter Parker is Spider-Man!'

Peter sat by Aunt May's bed all night. The next day MJ came to the hospital.

'How is she?' she asked Peter.

'She's going to be OK,' said Peter. 'Did you talk to Harry?'

'No, I didn't. The thing is … I'm in love with – don't laugh – Spider-Man.'

In her bed, Aunt May opened her eyes and listened.

'Oh, him,' said Peter. 'Well, he is very cool. I know him a bit. I take photos of him.'

'Does he talk about me?'

'Yeah. I talk to him about you. Once I said, "You know, Spider-Man, the great thing about MJ is – you look into her eyes and you feel stronger … excited … but frightened at the same time."'

'You said that?' MJ smiled and took Peter's hand.

Aunt May heard everything and she smiled, too.

The door opened quietly and Harry came into the room. MJ pulled her hand away but it was too late. They all knew.

Harry went to his father's home.

'You were right about MJ,' he said to his father. 'You're right about everything. She's in love with Peter.'

'Parker?' his father said quietly. 'And how does he feel about her?'

'Peter was in love with MJ when he was six! And he still loves her.'

Mr Osborn smiled. Then he looked at Harry sadly. 'I'm so sorry. I wasn't always there for you. But now things are going to be different. I'm going to make things right,' he said and took Harry in his arms.

Back at the hospital, Aunt May looked at Peter. Peter smiled back.

'A smile!' said Aunt May. 'And you smiled at MJ earlier today, too! You love MJ, Peter. Please tell her. Everyone knows you love her.'

But suddenly, Peter thought of the Green Goblin.

'Just a second, Aunt May,' he said and he left the room.

He called MJ's number but she didn't answer.

'MJ?' he shouted. 'Are you there?'

Then he heard a crazy laugh at the other end of the phone. 'Can Spider-Man come out to play?' It was the Green Goblin!

'Where is she?' Peter cried.

MJ woke up. It was night. She looked down. She was high up on the Queensboro Bridge. This was a bad dream, right? A cable car took people from Manhattan to Roosevelt Island. The lights were on in the cable car. She saw some children in the cable car. Then she heard a crazy laugh. It was the Green Goblin on his glider!

The Green Goblin shot at the cable car station on Roosevelt Island. The station exploded and the cable car stopped over the water.

Seconds later Spider-Man was there. Suddenly, there was a terrible sound. 'The cable is breaking,' thought Spider-Man. The cable car started to fall. 'I can't save them. There isn't time!'

Then the Green Goblin took the cable in his hand and saved the children! With the cable in his right hand, he glided up to MJ. He took her in his left arm and shouted, 'Spider-Man! Who is going to die? The woman you love or the little children? You choose!' And then the Green Goblin opened both his hands.

In a second, Spider-Man jumped down and took MJ in his arms. Then he took the cable in his other hand. He shot webbing at Queensboro Bridge and stopped the fall of the cable car.

Spider-Man said to MJ, 'Go down the cable to the cable car.'

'I can't.'

'Yes, you can, MJ.'

Slowly she went down.

Peter turned and the Green Goblin crashed into him. The Green Goblin laughed and turned the glider.

'It's time to die!' he cried and glided fast back under Queensboro Bridge. And then something hit the Green Goblin. The glider went around and around crazily. The people on the bridge shouted at the Green Goblin and hit him with bits from the bridge.

Carefully, Spider-Man put the cable car down onto a big boat under the bridge.

The Green Goblin shot a cable around Peter's body. Then he took Peter to an old building on Roosevelt Island. There, he hit Peter again and again.

'I'm going to finish MJ very slowly!' said the Green Goblin.

Peter looked up – he was angry! He hit the Green Goblin hard again and again. He shot webbing at a wall and pulled – it crashed down on the Green Goblin. At last, the fight was over.

'Peter, stop!' the Green Goblin cried. 'It's me.' He pulled off his mask. The tired face of Norman Osborn looked at Spider-Man.

'Mr Osborn …' said Peter.

'Peter …'

'Those OsCorp people are dead because of you.'

'No, that was the Green Goblin. Not me. You can save me, Peter. I'm like a father to you. Give me your hand …'

'I had a father. His name was Ben Parker.'

Peter's spider sense was working well. 'I can feel the glider behind me,' he thought. Suddenly, he jumped up high. The glider moved very fast. It glided right through Norman Osborn's body.

'Peter,' said Mr Osborn, before he died. 'Don't tell Harry.'

Spider-Man took Mr Osborn's body back to his house. Harry came into his father's room. He saw Spider-Man and the dead body.

'What did you do?' he shouted. But Spider-Man left quickly through the window.

## Chapter 9
## MJ's surprise

Harry was very sad and alone. Aunt May, MJ and Peter were there. Everyone was in black.

'I'm so sorry, Harry,' said Peter. 'It's difficult without a father. I know.'

'It was Spider-Man,' said Harry. 'My father is dead – and Spider-Man must pay.'

Harry looked at Peter sadly. 'You're the only family I have now.'

A little later, MJ and Peter talked together under some trees.

'Peter,' said MJ. 'I almost died on that bridge. But I thought about someone. And it wasn't Spider-Man … It was you, Peter.'

Peter smiled. 'Really?'

'The thing is … I love you, Peter. I love you so much.' She put her arms around him and they kissed.

Peter's love for MJ was strong. But it wasn't easy for Peter. He pulled away from her.

'There are things I can't tell you,' he said. 'But I'm always going to be there for you, MJ. I will always be your friend.'

MJ's eyes opened in surprise. 'Only your friend?'

'That's all I have,' answered Peter. And he walked away.

# FROM COMIC BOOK TO FILM

The world first met Spider-Man in 1962. It was in the comic book *Amazing Fantasy No. 15*. People loved him from the first day. But there were already other super-heroes around. Did the world need another one? Well, Marvel Comics thought so.

*Amazing Fantasy No. 15*

Spider-Man wasn't the same as other super-heroes. He was very strong but he also had problems. His readers had the same problems! And he lived in a great city: New York. Spider-Man is still many people's favourite super-hero.

**A Spider-Man comic from 1964**

**Who is your favourite super-hero? Why?**

Stan Lee thought of these names before he decided on 'Spider-Man':

Insect Man   Fly Man   Bug Man

Can you think of a name for a super-hero?

# SPIDER-MAN: THE FACTS

**1962** Stan Lee tells Marvel Comics he has an idea for a new super-hero – he shows them pictures of Spider-Man.

**1962** *Amazing Fantasy No. 15* is in the shops with the first Spider-Man story. Stan Lee writes it and Steve Ditko does the pictures.

**1967** Spider-Man is made into an animation. He's on TV for the first time.

**1977** A man plays Spider-Man on TV. But the show doesn't look great and the fans don't like it.

**1994** *Spider-Man: The Animated Series*. This was one of the best animated shows of all time. Spider-Man fans loved it.

**2001** Tobey Maguire stars as Spider-Man in cinemas all over the world. The film is one of Hollywood's biggest hits of all time.

What do these words mean? You can use a dictionary.
comic   super-hero   animation / animated   fan

# SPIDER-MAN AND NEW YORK

New York is a great place for Spider-Man. In Manhattan the buildings are tall and close together. He can jump and move quickly from building to building.

## 1 COLUMBIA UNIVERSITY

Peter's class come here at the beginning of the film. They visit the 'Genetic Research Institute'. Peter's life is never the same again!

## 2 TIMES SQUARE

In the film, the 'OsCorp World Unity Festival' happens here. There is a big street party in Times Square every year for New Year.

**You are going to New York for a holiday. Which places do you want to see?**

## 3 ROOSEVELT ISLAND CABLE CAR

This is the only cable car in New York. In the film, Spider-Man saves some children in the cable car. It's an exciting scene!

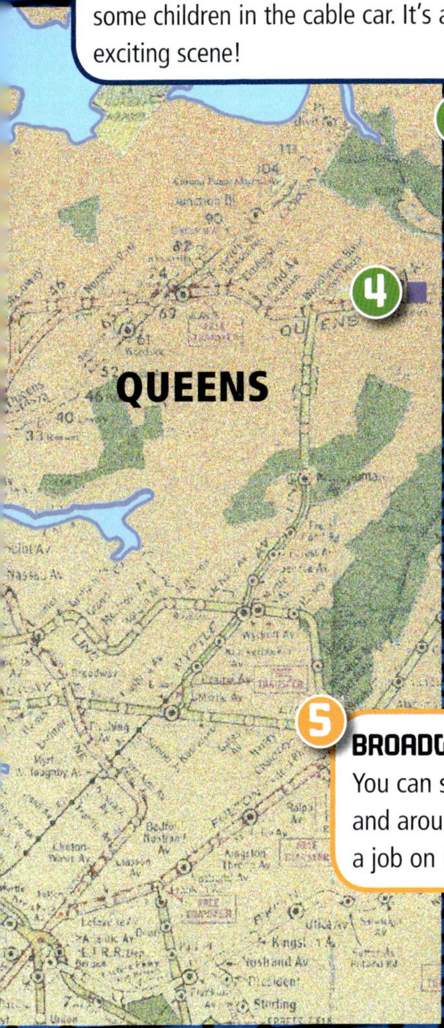


## 4 FOREST HILLS, QUEENS

Forest Hills is like an ordinary American town. Many New Yorkers live in Queens and work in Manhattan. Peter, MJ and their families live here.

## 5 BROADWAY

You can see lots of music shows and plays in and around Broadway. In the film, MJ wants a job on Broadway in a show or a play.

**What do these words mean? You can use a dictionary.**

**scene ordinary show**

# Thanksgiving

**In the film, Harry and Peter have Thanksgiving at their flat in Manhattan. Harry's father, MJ and Aunt May all come to the Thanksgiving meal. Peter arrives late and things go very wrong.**

## What is Thanksgiving?

It is a special day of the year in the USA. At Thanksgiving, Americans say 'thank you' for everything they have in their lives. It is always on the fourth Thursday in November.

## What happens at Thanksgiving?

It is a time for close family and friends to be together. The most important part of Thanksgiving is the special meal. The star of this meal is usually a big turkey with cranberry sauce. Usually all the food on the table is from North America, too.

**Do you have a special day like Thanksgiving in your country? What happens on that day?**

The first Thanksgiving

## When did Thanksgiving start?

Most Americans believe the first Thanksgiving happened in 1621 in Plymouth, Massachusetts. The Pilgrims and the Wampanoag people had a big meal together. They gave thanks for a good harvest.

## Who were the Pilgrims and the Wampanoag?

The Pilgrims were from England. They arrived at Plymouth on a boat called the Mayflower in 1620.

The Wampanoag people already lived in this part of America. They helped the Pilgrims and gave them food.

**What do these words mean? You can use a dictionary.**

meal turkey cranberry
sauce harvest balloon

## Did you know ...?

- Turkey is so important some Americans call Thanksgiving 'Turkey Day' or even 'T-Day'!
- Almost all of America's Thanksgiving cranberries (about 36,000,000 kilos) come from Buzzard's Bay, Massachusetts.
- In New York Macy's Thanksgiving Day Parade in Manhattan is very famous. Bands play music and everyone enjoys the party!

Macy's Thanksgiving Day Parade with big Spider-Man balloon!

# Chapters 1–3

## Before you read

1 Look at People and Places.

- **a)** Who lives in the house next to Peter?
- **b)** Who can run up walls?
- **c)** Who has a lot of money?
- **d)** Who isn't very good at science?
- **e)** How do you get from Manhattan to Queens?
- **f)** Where do the Parkers and the Watsons live?

2 Choose the right word. Use a dictionary.

**gas spider costume jump science**

- **a)** You can wear *this*.
- **b)** They teach you *this* at school.
- **c)** You can cook with *this*.
- **d)** *This* has eight legs.
- **e)** You do *this* to get down quickly from a high place.

## After you read

3 Choose the right words.

- **a)** Everyone at school wants to be friends with *Peter / Flash*.
- **b)** Peter changes because of the *spider / gas*.
- **c)** Dr Stromm's gas *is / isn't* ready.
- **d)** Peter *loves / hates* his new body.
- **e)** MJ comes from *a happy / an unhappy* home.
- **f)** Peter *did / didn't* stop the man with white hair.

4 Spider-Man can run up walls and fly from building to building. For one day you can be special, too. What special things can you do?

# Chapters 4–6

## Before you read

**5** Look at the New Words at the back of this book. Choose the right words for these sentences.

**a)** A … has eyes, arms and legs but is not a person.
**b)** Turn on a light in a room full of gas and it … .
**c)** When you are very frightened, you … loudly.
**d)** When something is wrong, Peter's … tells him.

**6** Answer the questions.

**a)** What jobs are Peter and MJ going to get after school, do you think?
**b)** Who is MJ going to go out with?

## After you read

**7** Answer the questions.

**a)** Life isn't easy for Peter after Uncle Ben dies. What makes him strong?
**b)** MJ says to Peter about her job in the restaurant, 'Don't tell Harry.' Why does she ask Peter this, do you think?
**c)** Peter works for the *Daily Bugle*. What does he do?
**d)** Why are Harry and MJ with the OsCorp people at the party in Times Square?
**e)** How does Spider-Man stop the Green Goblin in Times Square?

**8** Who says these things? Who to?

**a)** 'There's a room for you.'
**b)** 'There are worse jobs.'
**c)** 'You can have $200.'
**d)** 'You can't do this to me.'
**e)** 'Who are you?'

**9** Can you remember four things about the Green Goblin? Close your book and write them down.

# Chapters 7–9

**Before you read**

**10** Do you think the Green Goblin is finished? Who is the Green Goblin, do you think?

**After you read**

**11** Are the sentences right or wrong?

**a)** The Green Goblin wants to work with the *Daily Bugle*'s photographer.
**b)** Peter wants to take MJ out to a cheap burger bar.
**c)** Spider-Man saves an old woman from a fire.
**d)** There are four people at Harry's flat for Thanksgiving lunch.
**e)** The Green Goblin crashes into Aunt May's house because she is Peter's aunt.
**f)** MJ is in love with Peter.

**12** Put these sentences in the right order.

**a)** The Goblin puts the cable car onto a boat under the bridge.
**b)** Spider-Man takes Mr Osborn's body to his house.
**c)** Norman learns that Peter loves MJ.
**d)** Spider-Man catches the cable car and MJ.
**e)** The Goblin pulls off his mask
**f)** The Goblin puts MJ high up on a bridge.
**g)** The Goblin stops the cable car.
**h)** The Goblin takes Peter to an old building.
**i)** The Green Goblin takes MJ from her bed.

**13** What did you enjoy most in the story? Who did you like best?

**14** Work with another student. Write a different ending for the story.